COOL ON THE OUTSIDE
SCREAMING ON THE INSIDE

Published by CrankyBooks
Darien, Connecticut, USA
www.crankybooks.com

ISBN: 979-8-993528-2-0 (hardcover)
ISBN: 979-8-9935328-0-6 (paperback)
ISBN: 979-8-9935328-1-3 (eBook)

First Edition

Cover design by Lance Buckley
Printed in the United States of America

CrankyBooks
320 Boston Post Road
Suite 18-114
Darien, CT 06820

Written by Charles O'Neill
with editorial collaboration by Shannon Irving.

FAINT PRAISE FOR
COOL ON THE OUTSIDE, SCREAMING ON THE INSIDE

"I read this entire book on my date's phone at a
party I didn't want to be at. Ten out of ten."
—Your Friend Who's in a Band, so He Says

"Brand writes like someone who's been emotionally
abandoned by a therapist and turned it into a career."
—Anonymous Stranger, community
dining table, hotel in Hollywood

"This book made me laugh, then spiral, then laugh again.
I left it on my ex's nightstand. She hasn't texted back."
—Travis (no last name), definitely not doing great

"A deeply moving, emotionally unavailable book."
—The Barista Who Knows My Order but Not My Name

"Feels like watching a ceiling fan wobble at 3 a.m.
and thinking it knows your secrets. Five stars."
—Woman on the Subway with a Frizzy
Ponytail and an Oversized Sweater

"This book didn't change my life, but it did make
me feel seen—which I immediately denied."
—@broodingandunavailable, 1.1 million followers on Instagram

"The only book I've ever read that perfectly captures the
experience of being completely hollow in a flattering shirt."
—Mavrick's Uber Driver, five-star rating, no conversation

COOL
ON
THE
OUTSIDE
SCREAMING
ON
THE
INSIDE

BRAND MAVRICK
with CHARLIE O'NEILL

DISCLAIMER

This book satirizes cultural performance and the masks we wear in pursuit of "cool." It is a fictional work of social commentary focused on parodying lifestyle branding, image management, and the social rituals of looking composed.

All characters and events in this book are entirely fictional. References to real individuals or cultural figures appear only for purposes of satire and commentary. Apart from those intentional references, any resemblance to actual people, places, businesses, or events is purely coincidental. And if you think you recognize yourself or any other person, living or dead, you don't.

Nothing in these pages should be taken as advice on how to live your life. For that advice you should consult a professional—or your mom—or, failing that, your dog, who probably also loves you unconditionally.

Contents

Foreword

by Philbert T. Upton

Founding Partner, Panopticon Agency

Author of *Brands, like God, Require Faith*

I remember the first time I saw Brand Mavrick. He was leaning against a vending machine in the breakroom: black jeans, unreadable stare, earbuds in with no music. A lukewarm espresso in hand. Radiating absence like it was a choice.

Naturally, I hired him.

Over the years, Brand has taught me many things—none of them on purpose: that silence, when timed, can be a weapon; that a man can enter late, say nothing, and still win the meeting; that emotional distance almost guarantees a cult following on Spotify.

But most of all, he taught me that coolness—real coolness—is a trap designed to keep people far enough away that no one realizes you're unraveling. Which, in advertising, we call brand integrity.

This book is not a memoir. Brand wouldn't allow that much disclosure. It's not satire either; that would require admitting it's a joke. It's a mirror, angled so you wonder why your tote bag makes you feel less alone.

Read slowly. Take breaks. Hydrate. Cry into your hoodie if necessary. Just don't expect Brand to answer your email. He's already gone.

—Philbert T. Upton
Somewhere in Tribeca

Preface

I haven't always been this cool.

As a kid, I was awkward and raw. Windbreaker zipped to the chin. Haircut done at home. I used to hurl snowballs at my little brother Luke. One day, at the local skating pond, I hit him hard. Fastball, square to the face. We were both surprised, as I generally missed. No harm done, just a little slush under his Red Sox cap. Mrs. Brown, our fourth-grade teacher, saw the whole thing. She called my parents and said I had "some issues."

She had a point. But instead of digging into it, I made a decision. I was done with issues. No more problems. No angst, no mess, no distracting emotions. But how? Some kind of armor, maybe; a new identity.

I tried them on like jackets. The Hoods were recruiting—engineer boots, pocket blades, hair like black ice. I could've passed if I scowled. The Preppies were wearing madras shirts like they were blood types; sleeves rolled with surgical precision. They wore glasses they didn't need. The Rockers bebopped through hallways with radios welded to their ribs. Tempting—all of it. Then it hit me: Why pledge to a sub-tribe when the banner I wanted was the thing above them all? Cool. That's the mask I picked. Eventually it fit.

I couldn't define it then, but reading detective stories and watching Westerns had shown me that cool is quiet. It doesn't flinch. It walks into a room like it was there before you and then leaves without saying goodbye. That's what I wanted: to be untouchable.

People think cool is about style. In eighth grade, I thought that meant wearing fingerless gloves and quoting Ferris Bueller. Today, I am wearing black. But it's not some bold aesthetic statement. It's an opt-out. My color palette has the emotional spectrum of a fax machine. A few accessories, sure. Maybe a watch, the old Timex my dad gave me on my tenth birthday. Something that says, "I didn't try; I just am."

But the real work happens offstage: It's 2:07 a.m. The fridge is humming. You're standing there in your underwear, eating cereal out of the box. The breeze nudges the window curtain like it's checking in. That's the moment. That's where cool lives. Do you flinch? Do you narrate your own loneliness? Or do you just chew in peace?

Cool is staying upright when you're slipping. It's elegant survival; a stylish collapse you've folded like laundry. It's the ability to endure the absurdity of being human without flinching—to keep chewing your midnight cereal while the fridge hums like a low-budget therapist. Because true cool isn't external polish, but internal ease. It's how you inhabit yourself when the mask is off.

So yeah—these days, I'm cool. But, to get here, it took years of pretending not to care. Cool isn't inherited. It's not a gene or a birthright. And it sure as hell isn't that guy from high school who now sends emails about fantasy football and variable annuities with the subject line: "Great Opportunity!!!"

Becoming cool took time. It was learned. It was osmosis more than effort.

Those of us who yearned to be cool watched the ones who had it. The way they moved—never hurried or loud. Their jackets always fit. They didn't try. They just arrived. We noticed that cool people don't explain. They don't lead with a story about parking or traffic on the Merritt Parkway. They don't check their phones unless it's to end a conversation. They know that silence beats filling empty spaces with talk about the weather. They know that how you stand matters more than what you say.

So, we studied. We stole. We adapted. Some of us started spending time with cooler people. People with ice cube trays that made spheres. People who owned leather couches. People whose apartments had good lighting and who had opinions on vintage whiskeys. We picked things up. Tricks. Language tweaks. Posture adjustments. How to nod like you already knew. How to wear sunglasses indoors without appearing like you're part of an interpretive dance troupe that broke up last week.

Cool doesn't announce itself; it just shows up. You'll know it when you see it. Cool didn't just happen to people like me. It crept in sideways. Like starting to wear hats because your hair's thinning, and one day someone says, "That actually suits you," and boom—you're a hat guy now. Not by design. Just by survival.

Cool came through small choices, half-decisions you barely noticed. A pause before waving. A silence that lasted too long but somehow worked. It was a slow, strange evolution, a series of micro-decisions that didn't feel like much at the time: not talking just to fill the air, learning when not to care. By the time I was twenty, I'd figured out how to lean, how to exhale like I'd been there before, how to say nothing about a band unless they broke up right after I saw them in a one-off show in Berlin.

And eventually, I pulled it off: cool on the outside. But inside? Still that kid in the windbreaker, still wondering if Mrs. Brown was right.

There's a strange kind of pressure that comes with being composed. You become a mirror for other people's expectations. People assume you've cracked the code, that you've got it figured out. They don't see you eating cereal out of the box in the dark or standing in a grocery aisle staring at thirty-seven jars of peanut butter, forgetting why you're even there.

You become curated. Which is fine. Until it isn't. That's why this book exists. Not to fix it, just to name it. To say, "Here's what helps me stay together." Or to at least help you maintain the illusion long enough to survive another company offsite facilitated by a guy named Brad who uses too much hair gel, and where flip charts and sticky notes pass for vision. Coolness isn't a destination you reach. It's more like dental hygiene. Maintenance. Effort disguised as nonchalance.

So, in the chapters ahead, I'll walk you through my systems: how to stand at a party, how to dress without trying too hard, how to look like you've read something this month. You'll learn how to vanish just fast enough. How to maintain your mystique without becoming a sociopath. How to answer, "What do you do?" without spiraling.

Here's the deal: This isn't a self-help guide. It's not a manifesto. It's not for branding consultants or recovering theater kids. It's just a short, sharp list of things that have helped me retain a barely acceptable level of cool in the modern world without losing what's left of my soul. No need to take notes. Just read this like you're eavesdropping on someone you're not sure whether to admire or avoid.

We'll cover presence, absence, posture, texting, leaving early, staying too long, and putting yourself back together after a silent, internal collapse.

But not yet. For now, just stay with me.

—Brand Mavrick

In a slightly overlit rest-stop convenience store at a highway service area somewhere in Northern New England, 2:24 a.m., a bag of Bugles in my hand. The overhead lights are flickering. Trucks have surrounded the Blue Bird bus my parents converted into a motorhome in 1972. The scent of diesel brings back memories. And regret. Cool, but still figuring it out.

PART I

THE FOUNDATION
OF FAKERY

Social cool is walking
into a room like you
already regret it.
Office cool is walking
into a meeting
without planning
to take notes.

You've Entered the Room. Now What?

Scanning for Exits, Eyelines, and Internal Monologue Suppression

So. You're in.

The door has shut behind you with a sound like an accusation.

You're now officially inside—the restaurant, the party, the coworking space with succulents and self-actualized baristas. You've crossed the threshold from anonymity to possible humiliation. You know the feeling: that instant stomach drop like you just hit "Reply All" by mistake. Doesn't matter if it's a cocktail party or your cousin's wedding. Every doorway feels like a test you didn't study for. People are noticing you. Or worse, not noticing you. Either way, the panic is the same.

Let's break this down before you start sweating through your vintage tee. You're ready to scan the room like Mrs. Brown's about to grade you again.

Step 1: The Scan

You have three seconds to conduct the full Cool Guy Tactical Assessment:

1. Who's cooler than you? (Answer: everyone. Pretend otherwise.)
2. Where's the safest place to stand? (Answer: near something but not clinging to it.)

Do not

♦ hover near the buffet like an Oliver Twist extra

♦ pull out your phone too quickly (it'll look like you're waiting for someone to acknowledge you)

♦ talk to the host (just stay aloof and blame your therapist for your lack of eye contact).

Step 2: Invent a Backstory (Fast)

Being cool is 93 percent illusion and 7 percent how you hold your glass.

You didn't just stumble in here because a friend needed a wingman. Please. You're a low-key film editor who only cuts in black-and-white, a bikepacking minimalist who sleeps on gravel by choice, or a part-time philosopher who "just got back" from a silent retreat in Taos (where, obviously, you didn't speak but somehow found three new tattoo ideas).

> *Being cool is 93 percent illusion and 7 percent how you hold your glass.*

And when the inevitable, "So, where do you work?" lands, you don't answer—you deploy. Use one of these lines, polished to terrify and confuse:

- "I'm between roles, but it's intentional."

- "Mostly consulting. I can't really say much more."

- "I've been working on myself." (Nothing clears space at a party faster. Watch their pupils dilate, then retreat.)

Step 3: Choose Your Pose

Maybe you lean. Maybe you squint. One night I caught myself tapping my chin like I was calculating bond yields. That's how far I'll go to look unbothered.

Take your pick:

- **The Lean:** On a wall, bar, or exposed brick. Suggests calm detachment. Ideal for showcasing forearms.

- **The Squint:** Pretend you're reading something across the room. Preferably a soul.

- **The Half-Smile:** Shows irony and emotional withholding. Also prevents people from thinking you're approachable.

- **The Chin Tap:** Like you're trying to solve an existential crisis with a bad crypto tip.

Step 4: Fake One Connection

Find one person you already know or someone who looks insecure enough to accept your proximity. Walk up. Say something like, "Hey. Didn't we meet at that thing?" (There was no "thing." But now there is.)

The point isn't to make a friend. The point is to be seen being recognized, which is Cool Guy Fuel. Bonus: This shields you from wandering alone with a sweaty drink and no conversational landing pad.

Step 5: Establish Your Exit Strategy Immediately

Cool Guys are like vampires. They need to know how they're getting out before they go in. At any moment, you should be able to

♦ fake a call

♦ receive a sudden "client email"

♦ say you're heading to a second location (there is none).

Even your smile should say, "I'm here now, but I could leave, and you'd feel it."

Now breathe. Or don't. Up to you. You are now officially passing for cool. No truths told. No bonds formed. And safely concealed.

The slickest pitch I ever gave ended with the client saying, "That's clever, but what's it for?" My nasal huff said, "You just don't get it, but you wish you did." Confidence leaves the client impressed. Caffeination leaves them confused but alert.

Confidence vs. Caffeination

*Why You Mistake Anxiety for Charm—
and How to Weaponize It*

There's a fine line between self-assured magnetism and frantic, espresso-fueled mania, and you are straddling it like a man trying to do yoga in skinny jeans.

Let's be honest. You didn't walk into that place with "confidence." You walked in buzzing from a triple macchiato and a podcast in your ear telling you to "own the room." And maybe you told yourself this was the year you'd cut back. But then the barista said "oat milk" like it was destiny, and suddenly you were vibrating at a frequency only dogs can hear. Confidence? More like a cardiac event. You nodded. You clenched your jaw. You believed it. Inside? You were calculating whether there was enough Xanax left in the world to make small talk bearable.

So, what's the difference between confidence and caffeination? Let's compare the signals:

- Confidence makes eye contact, steady enough to unnerve your uncle at Thanksgiving. Caffeination? That's *too much* eye contact: no blinking, like a raccoon cornered by a flashlight.

- Confidence speaks slowly, with the pacing of someone reading bad poetry at a dive bar. Caffeination talks like a guy pitching crypto after three Red Bulls and a breakup.

- Confidence has nothing left to prove. Caffeination keeps explaining his "side hustle" until you start checking your cracked iPhone screen.

- Confidence is a slow burn. Caffeination taps his foot so hard it spells SOS in Morse code.

- Confidence is ordering a bottle of expensive champagne before your blind date shows up. Caffeination is the guy eating cold leftovers for dinner, replaying conversations in his head and rehearsing answers he'll never use.

The Great Confusion

Most modern guys weren't taught confidence. They were taught to perform, look sharp, act confident, and push through. That's not confidence. That's fight-or-flight in fitted clothing. But here's the secret sauce: You can use that caffeinated panic energy. You can shape it into something that looks like charisma. You just have to own the tremble.

Weaponizing the Buzz

Anxious energy, when framed correctly, comes off as "passion," "urgency," or my personal favorite, "an edge."

Here's how to channel it:

♦ *Break the fourth wall (quietly)*: Say something like, "I'm a little overstimulated, but that's just my default setting." Boom. You've disarmed your own jitteriness. You're no longer a mess; you're self-aware. That makes you dangerous. Mysterious. Cool, even.

♦ *Embrace controlled chaos*: Use your manic thought loops to your advantage. Be the guy with five hot takes in thirty seconds. Smile occasionally so they don't call security.

♦ *Use sudden stillness as a power move*: After a rapid-fire monologue, suddenly stop. Tilt your head slightly. Say something like, "But that's just how I see it." Then stare. Let the silence breathe, so they'll wonder if you're about to kiss them, fire them, or both.

♦ *Name your vices, casually*: Mention your caffeine dependence not as a flaw but as part of your brand: "I don't do mornings without a triple shot. I like my organs vibrating."

> *Confidence is a sustainable fire. Caffeination is a grease fire— impressive, flashy, and highly flammable."*

QUICK EXERCISE

Take This Personality Quiz

♦ *Do you feel confident right now?*

❑Yes

❑No

❑I've had two Americanos, and my heart just blinked.

♦ *What do you do when someone compliments you?*

❑I say, "Thank you."

❑I make a weird joke, and then deflect.

❑I black out and remember none of it.

♦ *What is your resting state?*

❑I'm chill.

❑I'm edgy.

❑I'm humming like a malfunctioning drone.

Remember: Confidence is a sustainable fire. Caffeination is a grease fire—impressive, flashy, and highly flammable. You're going to use it anyway. Just try not to burn down the house with you. (Also: Why did I even write a quiz?)

The uncoolest thing you can do in a meeting is explain the joke. The smirk works better. A smirk tells everyone you understood it all along, even if you didn't.

The Smirk That Hides a Thousand Cries

*Mastering the Disinterested Look
While Dying for Approval*

The modern man must maintain one essential facial expression at all times: the smirk. Just enough curve to suggest irony. Just enough detachment to imply, "I've seen things, but I'm not here to talk about them. Unless you beg."

Done correctly, the smirk says, "I'm above this conversation, but for some reason, I'm still here."

Done poorly, it says, "I just bit the inside of my cheek and I don't know what to do with my hands."

Let's get into it.

The Anatomy of the Smirk

To achieve the perfect smirk, follow these guidelines:

♦ *One corner only*: Two corners = a smile. A smile is vulnerable. Vulnerability is beautiful. Beauty is a liability. One corner only.

♦ Bonus: This also hides jaw tension from rage and your fourth espresso.

> *The modern man must maintain one essential facial expression at all times: the smirk.*

♦ *Dead eyes*: Your mouth can smirk, but your eyes must be emotionally unavailable. A true smirk requires the spiritual hollowness of a man who's just muted twelve Slack channels and forgot why he logged on. It's the look of a man who's opened too many tabs—browser tabs, emotional tabs, metaphysical tabs—and forgotten which one is playing music.

♦ *Micro tilt*: The head tilt suggests layered thought. It says, "I'm thinking something darker than I'm saying." You're not, but they don't know that.

♦ *Nostril tension*: A tiny flare, like you just remembered an unpaid parking ticket. It reads as judgment, which is all you really need in that moment. Perfect for when someone is explaining when AI will take over.

Situations That Call for the Smirk

Use the smirk if you find yourself in one of the following situations:

♦ *At a networking event*, someone says, "Crushing it." Apply a smirk and say, "Nice." They'll feel both affirmed and subtly roasted. That's power.

♦ *Your date* says, "I'm just figuring things out right now." Smirk. Nod. Say, "Aren't we all?" You've now displayed empathy without offering anything.

Practice Exercise: Mirror Work

Step in front of a mirror. No smiling. No laughing. Just the following inner monologue:

"Nothing you say will impress me. I want to go home. I'm lonely, but I can't say it. You fascinate me. I wish I were wearing a hoodie."

Now, lift one side of your mouth. Hold it. You're ready.

Advanced Technique: The Smirk and Redirect

Someone makes a joke. Everyone laughs. You twitch your lips but don't laugh. Then you say, "That reminds me of something I read recently ..." Boom. You've seized control while appearing not to care. If what you read doesn't exist, make it up. No one reads anymore.

Cautionary Tales: The Over-Smirk

Be careful. Overusing the smirk can result in the following:

- *Face freeze*: You'll look like a guy who's fresh out of his first encounter with Botox.

- *Resting condescension*: The face of someone who corrects pronunciation mid-conversation.

- *Permanent bachelor aura*: Your aura will repel intimacy like a citronella candle at a mosquito convention.

Final Thought

The smirk is a lie. But it's a useful one. It's the face you wear when your inner child is screaming, your inbox is pulsing, and your heart wants to be known—without cracking your myth of indifference

Smirk. Don't smile. That's the whole game.

Congratulations. You now look emotionally unavailable and deeply interesting. And that's cool.

Nothing ages faster
than a trend you
finally bought into.
Your carefully
curated shirt lies
so you don't have
to. It says, "I am
above trends."

Your Shirt Is Doing Most of the Work

A Visual Guide to Curated Nonchalance and Deodorant Layering

Clothes don't make the man. They just help the man disguise the fact that he hasn't felt genuine confidence since eighth grade, when he made someone laugh by accident and thought, "This is me now."

Fashion, for the modern emotionally constricted man, is not about expression; it's about armor. Your shirt is your narrative. Your jacket is your decoy. Your pants? They've given up, but we'll get there.

Your goal is to dress like someone who might have inner peace, while avoiding actual introspection.

The rule: If you're not cool yet, you can pretend a little, but carefully. Drop that story about how you almost shared a cab with Pete Davidson in New York but "the timing wasn't right." Maybe they'll nod politely, picturing you haunting some Brooklyn café with a single espresso and too many unspoken regrets. Maybe.

The Cool Guy Starter Kit

The Cool Guy's wardrobe must contain the following:

♦ *Neutral overshirt*: Says, "I'm low-effort, but also this cost $317." Pairs well with deliberate five o'clock shadow, brooding sound mix, disappointment.

♦ *Fitted tee with a faintly cryptic graphic*: A mountain. A bird. No words. Just vibes. Bonus if it's from a made-up festival or a defunct Japanese brand.

♦ *Jeans with one emotionally significant rip*: There's a rip in the knee, symbolizing vulnerability. You will not talk about it. But someone might notice.

♦ *Boots that look ready for a desert trek*: You won't hike, but you'll let them gather dust until one night you're buzzed enough to claim, "Yeah, I wore these when I camped at Joshua Tree." (You didn't. But the boots don't mind lying for you.) You want to suggest that you might hike if the right woman comes along and shows you a sunrise.

Deodorant Strategy: Layer like You Have Secrets

Cool Guys don't sweat; they leak mysterious scent notes that confuse and intrigue. The layering method:

1. *Basic deodorant*. Choose something that doesn't scream "locker room." You're not sporty. You're enigmatic.

2. *Subtle cologne, dabbed*—not sprayed—as if you skim *GQ,* but only for the layout.

Remember: *Detergent choice matters*. You want people to think your t-shirt smells like your essence, not the Costco laundry supplies aisle.

Your scent trail should make someone pause, inhale faintly, and think, "Who hurt him?"

Poses That Show off the Shirt, Not the Soul

Your shirt is the star of the show. You are just the reluctant vessel. Try these poses:

♦ *The Elbow Lean*: One arm up, one arm down. Casual sadness, artfully draped.

♦ *The Jacket Clutch*: Holding your outer layer like you're about to leave, but never do—well, except that one time. Commitment issues, rendered chic.

♦ *The Neck Tug*: One subtle pull at the collar. People will wonder if you're hot or haunted. (It's both.)

What NOT to Wear

The following should not be worn under any circumstances:

♦ *Anything that shows you tried*: Real cool is effortless. So, of course, you spent forty-five minutes crafting your outfit. But it shouldn't *look* like you did.

♦ *Shorts with too many pockets*: You're not prepping for a Boy Scout hike. You're carrying emotional complexity, maybe a half-written poem, maybe just a single gummy. Same difference.

♦ *Clothes with a slogan*: Your outfit should aim for ambiguity, not shout, *"ASK ME ABOUT MY STARTUP."*

> *Fashion, for the modern emotionally constricted man, is not about expression; it's about armor.*

Emergency Fashion Fixes

Cool Guys must always be ready to handle the following crises:

♦ *Feeling exposed?* Throw on a jacket. Any jacket. Even a questionable one. A jacket says, "I might disappear at any moment."

♦ *Sweaty?* Go with it. Say, "It's just the toxins leaving."

♦ *Someone compliments your outfit?* Deflect. Say, "Oh, this old thing?" (Even if you ordered it last night during a breakdown.)

Final Thought

Your clothes don't define you. But they can buy you just enough "modern cool" credit to ensure that you're the coolest person in the room—without even saying a word.

Advertisements and brand names are mirrors. We don't buy things—we buy the reflection we want to see. The people you loathe are just your reflection in bad lighting.

The Three Types
of Cool People
You Secretly Loathe

*A Field Guide to Aloof Tech Bros,
Soulful DJs, and Your Current
Girlfriend's Ex-Boyfriend*

There comes a moment in every man's private emotional unraveling when he looks around and thinks, "Why is that guy more relaxed than I am?" Spoiler: He's not. He's just faking it better. And worse: You hate him for it. And of course, you'll tell yourself it's not jealousy—it's anthropology. You're just studying the species in its natural habitat. But then why are you gripping your APSU Origin Water like it's the last parachute on a burning plane?

You know these guys. You hate them already.

> *You don't actually hate these guys. You hate that you think you're supposed to be these guys.*

The Aloof Tech Bro

- ♦ What he's also known as:

  - □ The Casual Prophet
  - □ The Algorithm Whisperer
  - □ The TED Talk Casualty

- ♦ How to spot him:

  - □ He wears $890 sneakers he calls "an investment."
  - □ He speaks in pitch deck metaphors: "We're pivoting to intentional living."
  - □ He acts like a man who's raised Series A funding for his personality.

- ♦ What infuriates you:

  - □ He stares into your eyes as though he's running internal focus groups on your social value.
  - □ He doesn't check his phone. His phone checks him.
  - □ He talks about biohacking but looks like he's never experienced malware of the soul.

- ♦ Coping strategy: Ask him one personal question: "Do you ever miss who you were before all the optimization?" He'll either short-circuit or start a Medium post about it.

The Soulful DJ

- What he's also known as:

  - The Vibe Curator
  - The Professional Mood Board
  - The Guy Who Says He Specializes in "Detroit-Inspired Techno with a Post-Industrial Twist" but Actually Only Does Weddings

- How to spot him:

  - He smells like incense and mild betrayal.
  - He dresses like a thrift store that had a nervous breakdown.
  - He makes direct eye contact while adjusting volume.
  - He's best known for once inserting three sad songs between "Shout" and the "Cha Cha Slide." He thought it made the night "deep." It didn't. It just made the bride forget to toss the bouquet.

- What infuriates you:

  - He speaks slowly, like every word is hand-poured over ice.
  - Women say he "just gets it," but he also gets away with ghosting like it's an art form.
  - He posts grainy selfies at dawn with captions like, "Found this light inside."

- Coping strategy: Pretend to confuse him with another DJ who's slightly more famous: "Weren't you at that thing in Berlin?" Even if he wasn't, he'll nod—because he needs you to believe it.

Your Current Girlfriend's Ex Boyfriend

- What he's also known as:

  - The One You Secretly Compete With
  - The Ghost of Confidence Past
  - That Bastard

- How to spot him:

  - The Ex-Boyfriend is rarely spotted. Instead, he's summoned. He exists in the way she once sighed at a Bon Jovi song, and in her cat, Mr. Fluffles (the Ex named him and the cat has never warmed to you).
  - He once backpacked across Iceland, and your girlfriend still follows him on Instagram because she "appreciates the artistry of his photos."
  - If he *is* spotted, he shows up at the bar in a linen shirt and a grin like he knows something you don't. Suddenly, you're competing with nostalgia itself.

- What infuriates you:

  - He's referenced just enough to matter.
  - It turns out he's the one who taught her how to make your favorite Moroccan dish.
  - He seems to have no visible wounds from the breakup.

- Coping strategy: Accept that you are fighting a hologram of her nostalgia. Then casually mention that you're "not really on social media anymore." You've just turned emotional detachment into a character trait. Victory.

BONUS: Composite Threat – The Tech DJ Ex

Occasionally, all three archetypes appear in one human form: a startup founder who also spins deep house and once dated someone you loved in college. Do not engage. Simply nod and back away slowly.

Final Thought

You don't actually hate these guys. You hate that you think you're supposed to *be* these guys. Here's the twist: They're screaming on the inside too (they've just built premium soundproofing). Stay cool. Or at least, stay intact.

PART II

ADVANCED SOCIAL SURVIVAL TACTICS

Cool in a meeting is asking the one question that makes half the PowerPoint irrelevant. If you're not the one who asked it, nod as if you already thought it. Every nod is a lie. The trick is making it look like folklore.

Nodding like You've Been Here Before

The Illusion of Belonging, Explained by a Guy Who Definitely Doesn't

Coolness is 80 percent posture, 15 percent fragrance layering, and 5 percent strategic nodding. That's it. That's the game.

Because here's the truth you already know in your bones: You don't belong here. But you also can't let anyone know that. Your mission isn't to be part of the scene; it's to nod like you've transcended the scene and are here for field research. Because nothing says "belonging" like pretending you don't belong. You become a human screensaver, just bouncing quietly around the edges of the place until someone mistakes your silence for wisdom.

Let's get you fluent in the silent, smug, deeply anxious language of Cool Guy Nodding.

The Social Nod Spectrum™

Let's be clear: None of this comes naturally. You practiced in elevators, in mirrors, maybe once in a Target parking lot while holding a LaCroix. Every nod you've ever given carries the weight of rehearsal. Which is fine—everyone else is faking, too. Just with better jawlines.

There are four major nods available to the modern man trying to fake belonging:

1. ***The Up-Nod (The "What's Up?"):*** A short upward tilt is best performed at a distance, across a conference table, or in a psychic void.

   - Used for
     - acknowledging other males without emotional entanglement
     - creating the illusion of mutual history
     - pretending you've seen this person perform stand-up once.

   - Caution: Too slow = threat. Too fast = needy. One beat. No bounce. No smile. The caffeinated nod buzzes like an overeager hummingbird. The confident nod says, "I see you, but I'd be just fine if I hadn't."

2. ***The Down-Nod (The "Respectful Dip"):*** A small chin-drop, often solemn. The ceremonial bow of male friendship.

   - Used for
     - greeting a model who pretends to remember you

- approving a DJ's track choice you don't actually know
- walking into any all-night diner wearing boots and the weight of unspoken regret.

- Bonus move: Pair with a half-closed eyelid squint, as if to say, "Yes. We are both aware of something deeper." (No one knows what. It doesn't matter.)

3. **The Loopback Nod:** You missed your chance, so now you're nodding too late.

- Used for
  - pretending you were just "lost in thought"
  - softening the sting of social oversight
  - offering a human moment without speech.

- Danger zone: If executed poorly, it looks like insecurity. If executed well, it looks like depth. I once loopback-nodded at a guy outside a 7-Eleven and he bought me a soda. To this day, I'm not sure if he thought I was cool or just thirsty.

4. **The Phantom Nod:** You nod at someone who didn't see it. You pretend you didn't either.

- Used for
  - humbling yourself
  - rehearsing real social interaction in your head
  - quietly reinforcing that you are, in fact, screaming on the inside.

How to Use the Nod to Create the Illusion of Familiarity

Here's how to execute the successful nod:

- Walk in. Don't smile. Nod once at someone. Even if you don't know them, they now assume you're connected to something (the art world, streetwear, a motorcycle cult no one's allowed to mention).

- Nod at a group without stopping. This makes you seem like a peripheral legend. You're known, but not bound by the rituals of conversation.

- Combine nodding with vague greetings: "Hey man," "Good to see you," "Been a minute." None confirm you know them. All imply history.

Practice Drill: The Mirror Nod Circuit

Set a timer and try each nod while holding direct eye contact with yourself. Then imagine performing them in these scenarios:

- You're at a party and see that guy from high school who won the lottery and now trades crypto full time "just for fun."

- You run into the woman you almost dated but who joined an underground kazoo orchestra in Peterborough, New Hampshire, before she joined you for dinner.

- You're greeted by a coworker whose name you still don't know.

If you can nod through those moments without flinching, you're ready.

Final Thought

Belonging is a myth sold to people who still believe in brunch. I'm not one of those people. Unless the brunch has all-you-can-eat waffles. Then, yes, I belong. You, my friend, are a nod-based organism, drifting silently through inhabited space, affirming nothing, admitting less. You don't need to be included. You just need to be remembered vaguely, and always with suspicion.

Cool in the office isn't sending long emails: it's sending five succinct words that say everything that needs to be said. The lean is the physical version of that.

7

Strategic Leaning: Barstools, Brick Walls, and Casual Despair

Body Language for the Emotionally Unavailable

L eaning is survival. Standing tall is for people who believe in themselves. You don't. Not really. You believe in angles. Angles let you vanish, let you seem like you're in mid-thought when you're actually just meditating. You might think posture is about comfort. It's not. It's a social signal. A declaration. A performance of detachment that is carefully staged for maximum effect. And no posture says, "I could leave at any moment, but won't," quite like the Strategic Lean. It's how the modern man says, "I'm not part of this. But I'm here. And somehow that counts."

Why We Lean

Let's be honest: Standing upright with purpose implies too much intention. You're not here with goals. You're here with vague longing, unresolved father issues, and a hope that someone will see you and say, "He looks like he's been through something."

The lean is your shield. You're not leaning because you're tired; you're leaning because standing upright feels like a confession. Better to hope someone mistakes it for emotional gravity instead of weak quads. You plant one limb on something solid—a wall, a counter, a railing—as if to say, "This is where I belong now. I'm part of the architecture. But emotionally."

The Five Leaning Archetypes

Now that you've learned *why* we lean, let's take a look at *how* to lean:

1. ***The Brick Wall Lean:*** Classic. One shoulder pressed lightly against a weathered surface. Hands in pockets. Head tilted like you just remembered a betrayal.

   - Used for
     - outdoor gatherings
     - introspective cigarette moments (even if you don't smoke)
     - watching someone you once loved laugh with someone whose haircut cost more than your rent.

   - Warning: Too much pressure = desperation. This isn't a crutch. This is a prop.

2. ***The Barstool Slouch:*** Back against the bar. One elbow against the rail. Legs crossed just enough to imply jazz, sorrow, or divorce.

   ◆ Used for
     □ late-night rambling that feels profound
     □ pretending you're not waiting for someone to text back
     □ posing like you're not posing.

   ◆ Bonus move: Sip slowly. Examine the ice like you're solving a small mystery inside the glass.

3. ***The Mirror Lean:*** You're not looking at yourself. You're looking past yourself, into the abyss. Which, conveniently, is behind you.

   ◆ Used for
     □ dimly lit ramen counters and gloomy tapas bars
     □ buffet tables at parties you regret attending
     □ practicing micro-expressions of pain and allure.

4. ***The Two-Handed Sink Grasp:*** Also known as The Quiet Breakdown Lean. You lean in, let the water run, stare at your reflection. You're not washing your hands; you're symbolically rinsing off the burden of being misunderstood. Last time I did it, a guy walked into the men's room and said, "Rough night?" I nodded. He didn't know I was only hiding from the soggy buffet shrimp that the guy at the next table kept telling me I "must try."

- Used for
  - the bathroom at a greasy burger joint that's made you question all of your life's decisions
  - offices with bad lighting and even worse morale
  - moments when someone says, "You okay, man?" and you reply, "Just tired."

5. ***The Frame Lean:*** Leaning inside a doorway, against a car, or beside a large industrial window. Framed. Beautiful. Doomed.

- Used for
  - looking like you're about to leave
  - looking like you were never really here
  - looking like someone who once told someone else, "Don't wait up!"

6. ***Avoid: The Buffet Lean:*** Propping yourself against a folding table with raw oysters you don't trust. No one respects this lean. Don't be this guy.

Mastering the Lean-to-Leave Transition

You've leaned long enough. It's time to leave, or at least threaten to. The key is slow movement, as if your body is made of memory foam and doubt. Say, "I should probably head out." But stay. This is the language of the emotionally unavailable.

Quick Tips for Lean Realism

Follow the below tips for a flawlessly executed lean:

♦ Don't switch leans too fast. This shows panic.

♦ Avoid chairs that creak. Nothing kills gravitas like a squeak that says, "Office Depot."

♦ At least on Tuesdays, look like you're watching something—even if it's the last flicker of your self-esteem.

Final Thought

Leaning is not about resting. It's about making the world hold some of your weight while you pretend to carry the rest effortlessly. In a culture obsessed with movement, leaning becomes a kind of quiet resistance; it whispers, "I will not stand up for you."

Cool is the colleague who doesn't roll their eyes during the tenth team update of the week. That's the same restraint you need for laughter: Keep it sealed. The less joy you show, the more mysterious you seem.

Laughing Without Showing Teeth

*Because Joy Is Weakness, and
Molars Are Vulnerability*

L aughter is dangerous. Real laughter exposes things: delight, surprise, and, God forbid, hope. And nothing ruins a carefully curated Cool Guy persona faster than revealing you're actually enjoying yourself.

So instead, we've evolved a workaround: the toothless laugh. A smile's older, sadder cousin. It's the tight-lipped chuckle that says, "I see the joke. I'm just not letting it in." It's like when someone sends you a meme you saw three days ago. You can't laugh. That would be dishonest. But you can't ignore it either. So, you settle for that faint nasal exhale that says, "I acknowledge humor exists, but not for me. Not tonight."

Why no teeth? Teeth are primal. They say, "I feel safe," "I trust you," "I forgot, for a moment, how broken everything is." Which means no teeth. Ever. Besides, teeth are forever tied to dentists, and dentists to childhood trauma, and trauma to therapy you didn't actually go to. Keep it closed. Keep it tight. A sealed mouth says, "I know the joke, but my molars are under NDA." You want to laugh like someone who heard a better joke on the subway while crying into a paper bag.

The Three Approved Laugh Types for the Modern Cool Male

For maximum coolness, only the following laughs are acceptable:

1. **The Nasal Huff:** A brief exhale through the nose. No smile. No eye squint. Just a faint puff, like disappointment escaping a deflating balloon.

   - Used for
     - a friend's joke you don't actually understand
     - your date's story about their therapist.

   - Translation: "I'm technically amused, but I'm better than this moment."

2. **The Ghost Chuckle:** Mouth closed. Shoulders bounce once.

   - Used for
     - group settings where you don't want to be noticed
     - conversations with people you may need to ghost
     - jokes made by people more attractive than you.

   - Translation: "I'm smiling on the inside, but only to stop myself from screaming."

3. ***The Crooked Grin with Delayed Head Shake:*** The smile that dies halfway across your face.

- ◆ Used for
  - ▫ when you realize you could fall for this person, and that terrifies you
  - ▫ when someone quotes a show you pretend not to watch
  - ▫ when someone makes a genuinely good joke, but you refuse to surrender. Bonus points for a slow head shake, like you're disappointed the world still has the nerve to be funny.

- ◆ Translation: "You got me. But not all of me."

Dangerous Laughs to Avoid

Do not ever use the following uncool laughs:

- ◆ ***The Full-Teeth Laugh or Full-Teeth Cackle:*** Exposes molars and vulnerability. It makes you look like someone who still believes in magic shows.

- ◆ ***The "HA!" Outburst:*** Sudden, authentic joy? Not in this economy.

How to Respond to Genuinely Funny People (Without Compromising Your Cool)

The Cool Guy cannot, under any circumstances, reveal that he thought that something was funny. If you find yourself in that precarious situation, respond to the comic offender in one of the following ways:

- *Stare at them while sipping something.* This suggests that you find their humor interesting, but not energizing.

- *Say, "You're ridiculous," while refusing to laugh.* It's the humor equivalent of giving someone a key to your apartment but insisting you're still just friends.

- *Use the one-eyebrow raise.* This signals appreciation with just a hint of judgement. Perfect.

Emergency Deflection Technique for When Your Laughter Almost Escapes

In a worst case scenario when you almost let a genuine laugh slip, you should immediately

- cough

- sip

- look at your phone

- change the subject to something like, "Anyway, I've been thinking about how nothing we do will really be remembered ..." Now you're the mysterious one.

Final Thought

To laugh openly is to say, "This moment matters." And that, friend, is not on brand. So instead, you smile like a man guarding a secret. You chuckle like it costs something. And you carry on, unreadable and vaguely amused—the human version of a shrug in a leather jacket.

The mall is a church for people who want salvation at 40 percent off. Consumer brooding is just prayer with a receipt.

Brooding in Public Spaces: The Art of Performing Depth

Where to Sit, What to Sip, and How to Look like You're Processing Trauma

Brooding is essential. It's how you communicate to the world that, yes, you could be enjoying this overpriced flatbread with figs and arugula, but you're also carrying the weight of veiled tragedies and emotional epiphanies.

You don't need to be deep. You just need to look like someone who's recently considered the impermanence of love.

What Is Brooding?

Brooding is not sulking. Sulking is what toddlers do when they don't get more juice. Brooding is a mature, curated melancholy—a quiet theater of inwardness, presented in public, for strategic effect. You don't even need to feel sad. You just need to look like you could be. That's the trick. Other people will fill in the gaps with their own projections. You're an empty slide projector; they're the film. You get credit for depth without lifting a finger. Lazy, yes. Effective, also yes. It's existential marketing: "I'm not available right now. I'm processing."

No one knows what you're processing. That's the point. And if someone did ask, you wouldn't tell them. You'd just shrug like you're carrying a metaphorical piano up a flight of emotional stairs, but quietly.

Top-Rated Brooding Locations

Brooding, like real estate, is all about location. Choose wisely:

1. **_The Coffee Shop Window Seat:_** You stare outside, slowly slip your lukewarm espresso, and pretend to highlight a book you know you won't finish (ideally, something printed in runes or a dead language only a few scholars can read; or, failing that, maybe _Ulysses_). Once, I tried brooding with an actual highlighter. The pink streak on my face didn't exactly scream "depth." Lesson: Props shouldn't stain.
   ◆ Occasional moves:
      □ Remove your glasses and rub your eyes like the truth hurts.
      □ Look up at nothing, as if the clouds remind you of her.

2. **The Park Bench near a Fountain:** You're surrounded by joy. Children laugh. Couples walk hand in hand. But you? You sit like a man revisiting a personal war.
   - Outfit tip: Wear a long coat in spring. Bonus points if it's thrifted and smells faintly of rain and a special place you left too soon.

3. **The Subway Platform:** Brooding at its purest. No Wi-Fi. No eye contact. Just you, a steel pillar, and the aura of someone else's unease.
   - Recommended accessories:
     - wired earbuds you refuse to replace (nonfunctional = deeper pain)
     - an unread text from your mother

4. **The Expensive Hotel Café:** This one's elite. You brood against the noise. You sit at the corner of the family-style table, your small plate of quail eggs with caviar untouched. You're surrounded by movement, and yet you remain still, unreachable. People wonder: Is he sad? Or enlightened? You're thinking: Can they pack the quail eggs and caviar to go? And has it really come to this?

Brooding Poses
(Ranked by Despair-to-Hotness Ratio):

These poses say, "I'm brooding" out loud so that you don't have to:

1. *Forearm-to-Forehead Lean*: Pure poetry. Do not overuse. May trigger concern.

2. *Eyes-Closed Head Tilt*: Looks like meditation, but it's just exhaustion.

3. *One-Foot-on-the-Wall Lean*: For outdoor brooding only. Screams, "I've seen things."
   - *Avoid*: Crying. That's not brooding—that's catharsis. Catharsis is too real.

Conversation Snippets to Be Overheard

Say quietly, without explanation:

- "I just think timing ruins most things."

- "There's beauty in not needing answers."

- "No, it's not about her. It's bigger than that."

Then look into the middle distance like you've already died once.

Brooding Music: Ambient Sad Vibes Only

You'll need a playlist titled something like:

- Ghost in My Hoodie

- Smiling Is a Lie

- Songs for Looking Away When People Laugh

Make sure there's at least one song in French. Even if you don't understand it. Especially if you don't.

Final Thought

Brooding isn't about depression. It's about aesthetic sorrow. A type of visible emotional residue that clings to you like smoke from a fire that might still be burning. Brooding is just ghosting in public. Sitting still so no one notices you've already left. You are the guy they write breakup songs about—even if you never texted back. Especially then.

Congratulations. You've achieved a portable mystique.

PART III

MAINTAINING THE MASK

Advertising is the art
of helping consumers
mistake packaging
for products. Your
questions should
work the same
way: empty box,
shiny wrapping.

Questions to Ask
That Sound Smart
but Reveal Nothing

The Art of Conversational Smoke Bombs

ool is not about answers. It's about questions, the kind that drift into the air like incense and leave everyone wondering if they missed something.

The modern emotionally guarded man doesn't explain himself. He simply tosses a cryptic inquiry into the mix, like a flash grenade made out of philosophy and unresolved personal baggage.

Why Ask Questions That Reveal Nothing?

Because once you start sharing facts, people think they know you. And knowing leads to expectations. Suddenly you're not just the mysterious guy at the diner; you're the guy who has to help someone move on Saturday. That's not cool. That's manual labor. And you don't want to help.

Help is messy. Help means change, and change means work. You're not here for work. You're here to drop conversational grenades, nod solemnly, and then disappear like you're allergic to intimacy.

Your questions should suggest: intelligence, wounds, late-night journaling. You must be interesting, unfixed, and just aloof enough to be alluring.

The Top Ten Cool Guy Questions (That Go Nowhere)

The ten questions below are gold. Study them:

1. *"What's your take on all this?"* No context. No topic. Just "this." Let them define it. Whatever they say, nod like you were thinking the same thing. Then glance at the ceiling like you're listening to ghosts.

2. *"Do you think people can actually change?"* Someone once told me, "Yes, of course." I nodded, pretended to agree, then went home and rearranged my books for the fifth time that month. Change? Technically. Growth? Questionable.

3. *"What's something you haven't told anyone?"* Power move. You give nothing back. If they answer, you win intimacy without risk. If they hesitate, you display a half-curled grimace like you already know.

4. *"Where do you feel most like yourself?"* Follow up with silence. Let the weight of the question do the work while you sip something dark and overpriced, ideally in a tiny glass.

5. *"Do you ever wonder if any of this is real?"* Best deployed when
   * looking out a window
   * lying on a couch sideways
   * hearing someone say they love their job
   * scrolling Zillow at 3 a.m. for houses you'll never buy.

6. *"Have you ever felt completely seen?"* Used to destabilize dates and earn hugs from strangers. Pro tip: After they answer, look down and whisper, "Yeah. Me neither."

7. *"Do you think we're all just running from something?"* No one will say no. You've just created a false sense of shared trauma.

8. *"What's your definition of freedom?"* Don't answer your own question. Just let them talk. Bonus if you nod like you were briefly imprisoned.

9. *"What's the one question you're afraid someone might ask you?"* If they flip this back on you, say, "Exactly." You've just said nothing—perfectly.

10. *"If you met yourself at a party, would you stay or make an excuse to leave?"* This is a mirror disguised as small talk. The brave ones answer. The rest check their phone, mumble something about an early meeting, and disappear before you can say "fair."

None of these questions lead anywhere. That's the point. They're conversational smoke bombs you drop to look mysterious while you stall for an actual thought. They won't make anyone bond with you. But they *might* make them text you later, just to figure out what the hell you meant. Ask questions often. Answer them rarely. And if someone ever gives a really good answer? Congratulations. You've just met your emotional twin. Now you'll be thinking about it for weeks.

How to Exit a Conversation After Deploying a Deep Question

You don't stick around for resolution. That's not cool; that's closure. Instead:

- Glance at your phone or watch. (Bonus if you have neither with you.)

- Say, "I should probably head out, but this was ... meaningful."

- Fade into the background like the closing scene of *Eraserhead*.

Final Thought

Words are tools. But questions are smoke. They obscure, distract, and elevate. And in the fog of your controlled ambiguity, people will mistake curiosity for depth. Remember: It's not about being understood; it's about being misunderstood in a beautiful way. Anyway, ask questions. Don't answer. That's enough.

The trick to surviving a bad boss is letting them think your idea was theirs. Ghosting works the same way: Leave them thinking the connection was theirs to lose. Ghosting is just brand management for your soul.

When Someone
Gets Too Close

Deploying the Well-Timed Ghost

There comes a moment after the playlist has faded, after the party has ended, after someone opens the vault to their childhood trauma like it's a photo album, when the modern Cool Guy feels a chill in his core. Someone is getting close. They've asked a real question. They've used your name. They've started hoping for something. This is when you must act. Not with honesty. Not with vulnerability. But with the well-timed ghost; the elegant exit of a man who refuses to be healed.

Why Ghosting Isn't Cruel *(It's Just Efficient)*

Let's reframe this. You're not avoiding connection. You're preserving your mystique. You're protecting the version of yourself that seemed charming, present, vaguely tormented. The one they found intriguing before you said something emotionally earnest about your dad.

You are not a jerk. You are a concept. Concepts don't pay rent. Concepts don't buy groceries. Concepts drift through conversations like cigarette smoke in a movie where no one ever coughs. That's you now: cinematic, but useless. And concepts don't reply to texts. At least that's what you tell yourself at 3:07 a.m. while holding the phone, debating whether to type "thinking of you."

You're not cruel. You're just unfinished. You're still in beta. Let them test the stable version of someone else.

Ghosting, Ranked by Intensity

When looking to ghost, choose one of the following techniques:

1. **The Soft Fade:** You slowly become less available. Texts go from playful to purely time-stamped. "Ha." "Busy." "Raincheck." Eventually, you become someone who once meant something. You become background noise. Familiar, but no longer pressing play.

2. **The Calendar-Based Vanish:** You say you're "traveling." "Off-grid." "Going through something." Last time I tried it, I accidentally posted a photo of my dog sleeping on my couch on Instagram. She texted, "Off-grid, huh?" I deleted it, but the damage was done.

3. **The Technological Collapse:** Your phone broke. Your app glitched. Your account was hacked by Russian bots or crypto scammers. You reappear weeks later with a simple message: "lol just saw this." Then nothing—like a ghost with a data plan.

4. **The Full Fade to Myth:** No warning. No trace. You were a beautiful idea in their life, like brunch plans or the notion of closure. One day, they'll say, "He just ... disappeared." And someone else will whisper: "Legend."

Signs It's Time to Ghost

These are the five-alarm fires that it's time to ghost:

♦ They make you a playlist. Get out. That's practically a subpoena.

♦ They want to introduce you to their therapist or their family.

♦ They say things like, "I feel safe with you."

♦ You hear yourself say, "I really like you," and immediately fantasize about fleeing to a faraway city you haven't been to.

These are your evacuation sirens. Pack your silence and go.

The Ghost's Code of Conduct

You may be cool. But you're not heartless. Follow these guidelines:

♦ Ghosting someone mid-vulnerability is cruel. Wait at least twelve hours—or one sleep cycle—after they've shared a trauma.

♦ Don't leave them hanging mid-date. Leave the moment after you say something cryptic like, "This feels too real." If they confront you, pretend to be confused: "Wait ... I thought we were just ... vibing?" Let them think they imagined the connection. It's cleaner that way.

What to Say If You Accidentally Run Into Someone You've Ghosted

It's the day you hoped would never come. Here's how to handle it:

- "Hey. Wow. It's been ... time, huh?"

- "You look ... different. In a good way. I think."

- "I was just thinking about you. Strange, right?"

Then smile like you've been living in a cabin. Even if you've just been doomscrolling on the couch in your apartment.

Final Thought

Ghosting isn't about escape. It's about preserving the illusion that you were never fully here to begin with. You are a fog machine in human form. A memory with cheekbones. An "almost." Coolness isn't presence. It's the afterglow of absence.

When I told HR my workload was overwhelming, they offered resilience training. It was a PowerPoint with stock photos of people climbing mountains. Often, therapy teaches only one thing: how to smile while burning out

Therapy as a Vibe, Not a Process

How to Mention Therapy
Without Ever Going

In modern culture, therapy is currency. You don't need to do it. You just need to reference it vaguely and convincingly, like a guy who definitely owns a passport but only uses it to flirt. Because actually going to therapy? That might involve effort. Or growth. Or crying with intention, which has been outlawed under the Brooding Convention of 2017.

Why Talk About Therapy?

Saying, "I'm in therapy" does three important things:

1. It signals emotional awareness without confirming emotional health.
2. It creates the illusion of progress while you stay unchanged.

3. It makes you appear safe, but not so functional that anyone would actually rely on you.

It's like saying, "I know I'm a mess. But I'm a self-aware mess." Self-awareness is the new cologne; everyone sprays it. You don't have to be fixed, you just have to know you're broken in the right lighting. Post a vague story, mutter about your "work in progress," and boom: you're enlightened. It's yoga for people who can't touch their toes.

Approved Therapy Phrases That Imply Depth (Without Commitment)

Use these casually in conversation (and do not elaborate):

- ♦ "My therapist once said something about that ..."
- ♦ "We've been unpacking a lot of this lately."
- ♦ "It's wild how it all ties back to childhood, right?"
- ♦ "I journal after sessions. It's helped ... kind of."
- ♦ "I ghosted my last therapist. Still unpacking that."

Trail off mid-sentence. Let your silence suggest layers.

Strategic Therapist Inventions

If you haven't been to therapy but need a therapist on standby, create a fictional one with these four attributes:

1. **Gender-neutral name:** Alex, Taylor, Jordan
2. **Located somewhere inconvenient:** "Hard to schedule. They're based in Vermont and refuse to use Zoom."

3. **Described in contradictions:** "Tough but warm," "Clinical but amusing," "Speaks in metaphors, but also deadpans."

4. **Spiritually ambiguous:** "Now they're into sound baths." Boom. Unverifiable and impressive.

Situations Where You Should Reference Therapy

Mentioning therapy is powerful in the following circumstances:

♦ **During a breakup:** "My therapist told me I sabotage myself when I get close to real joy." Then look down and breathe like you almost didn't say it.

♦ **When someone asks about your past:** "That's still a work in progress." Smile like you're both sad and proud.

♦ **When asked what you're doing this weekend:** "There's this therapy thing Saturday morning, then probably just reading." They won't question it. You've just booked a fake weekend of emotional labor.

♦ **When your boss asks why you missed a deadline:** "My therapist said I have to start setting boundaries." Instant moral authority.

Mistakes to Avoid

Failure to pay attention to the following rules will result in the loss of some cool points:

- *Do not quote influencers*. You're not on Instagram. You're in crisis.

- *Do not overexplain*. If you sound fluent in CBT terminology, they'll know you've only read one infographic.

- *Do not say*, "Mental health is important" too loudly. This screams "LinkedIn post," not "man in healing."

What If You Actually Need Therapy?

That's not our department. But if you ever go, just know: maybe it will help you. But if not, you'll become the kind of person who can say, "Yeah, I've done the work," even if you're still screaming inside—you're just screaming more mindfully.

Final Thought

Therapy is not always a tool for healing—it's a vibe. You're not broken; you're fractured in an expensive way. You're a man in progress.

Cool is understanding that internet radio algorithms are like drunk DJs who only play the songs you hate. So, you curate your own playlist full of songs you hate or have never heard before. That way, you're in control, and you're ironic, which is so, so cool.

Curating Your
Emotional Playlist
(Without Ever Listening to It)

*How to Broadcast Longing While
Remaining Completely Unavailable*

Music reflects the soul. But for the modern Cool Guy, it's camouflage designed to look like feeling without the burden that goes with actual emotional participation.

You don't *feel* your playlist. You imply that you've felt things, once, in another country, under fog. Your goal is not catharsis. Your goal is to haunt someone's Bluetooth speaker long after you've ghosted them. And honestly? Half the songs you add, you skip after ten seconds. But that doesn't matter. No one ever listens all the way through—they just scroll the track list. You're not building an actual listening experience; you're building an identity résumé. Music is LinkedIn for vibes.

Why Create a Playlist You Don't Listen To?

The role of the playlist is to

♦ attract people who say, "This is a vibe" when they see it posted online

♦ hint that you cry, but only in cinematic lighting

♦ make someone wonder what happened to you in 2019

♦ ensure that if you die mysteriously, your playlist becomes your eulogy.

What to Include

A proper Emotional Playlist should contain each of the following four tracks:

1. **The Obscure Opening Track:**
    ♦ It should be a slow burn by an artist no one knows (preferably Icelandic).
    ♦ It's ideally lo-fi and recorded on what sounds like a cassette player inside a snowstorm, or maybe a washing machine. Hard to tell. That's the point.
    ♦ It says, "If you know this, we can date. But I'll still disappear."

2. **The Sad-Boy Anthem:**
    ♦ It should be a track with whispered vocals and a title longer than your last relationship. Mine was called, "Don't Cry for Me, I'm Already at the Waffle House." I played it for a date once. She asked if it was a parody. It wasn't. I still don't know if she's recovered.

- This track is your secret weapon. It plays at volume level three while you work. You hum along like it reminds you of someone you once kissed during a blackout and later wrote a poem about.
- Requirements for the Sad-Boy Anthem are as follows:
  - It has minimal instrumentation.
  - Its lyrics reference rain, Polaroids, staring at a ceiling, or a corduroy jacket someone left at your house in 2007.
  - It should feel like a metaphor. If someone hears you listening to it, lock eyes with them and say, "It's such a testament to the tension between marriage and late-stage capitalism, you know?" Then look away. Do not engage any further.

3. ***The Song That Suggests You Are Artsy and Complex:*** Ideally from the soundtrack of an arthouse film you always recommend but have never actually seen.

4. ***The One Rage Track You Don't Explain:*** Screaming, distortion, chaos. Toss it in at track eight. Let people wonder what happened. Let them fear they'll have to hear it again.

Playlist Title Hall of Fame

Your playlist must have a title that sounds like at least one of the following:

- a breakup note

- a philosophy thesis

- a deleted text message

- a dream you woke up from, sweating

Examples of playlist titles:

- Songs for the Days I Don't Reply

- Was It Always like This

- If You Read This I'm Sorry (But Not Really)

- Almost Morning, Still You

- Untitled // Healing

- Noise Between Lovers

Never explain your title. If someone asks, just exhale and say, "It's complicated. You wouldn't understand."

Sometimes I scroll through my own playlist names and wonder if past-me was in on the joke, or if he actually believed those titles mattered. Probably both. Probably neither. Who knows? That's the beauty of it: People will assume intention when there is just insomnia.

Sharing Strategies

You've curated your perfect playlist. Now it's time to introduce it to the world. Choose one of the following strategies:

- Post it to Instagram with no caption, just the link. Then promptly delete it. Mystery restored.

- Send it to someone at 1:11 a.m. with, "This made me think of you." Then never respond again.

What You Don't Include

The following tracks on your playlist are the cool kiss of death. Do not include

♦ upbeat music

♦ anything too confident or optimistic

♦ anything your mom could sing along to

♦ songs that people actually dance to (this isn't a party; it's a slow emotional collapse with rhythm).

Final Thought

Your playlist isn't just music. It's emotional theater. A curated ache, looping forever, long after you've logged off. People don't hear your songs; they inherit your ghost. Let people think your playlist is a rare peek into your beautifully damaged mind. You're mysterious, esoteric, and so, so cool.

Cool is convincing consumers to buy consumers to buy sneakers named after a man who wouldn't let them in his limo. Accessories are the same scam: sell the story, not the item. Accessories don't finish the outfit; they finish the scam.

Accessories That Say, "Ask Me About My Inner Turmoil"

How to Dress like Someone Who's Barely Holding It Together—Beautifully

Anyone can wear clothes. But only the emotionally elusive man knows how to accessorize his neuroses. Accessories aren't just additions; they're statements. They whisper, "I have felt things," "I may still be healing," "I might talk about it. But not here. Not now. Maybe never."

Mystery works better than honesty. My ring? Bought at a kiosk during a layover in Denver. My bracelet? Found in a CVS clearance bin. But no one needs to know that. Mystery implies vintage souvenirs from a solo cross-country road trip. Your job isn't to reveal your story. Your job is to decorate the void.

Core Accessory Traits for the Brooding Elite:

The right cool accessories have the below four traits:

1. *They are worn but intentional.* Nothing too new.
2. *They are suggestive of a backstory.* Bonus if it belonged to "someone who mattered."
3. *They are slightly out of place.* Like you.
4. *They are impractical.* Function is for people who aren't doing shadow work.

Approved Accessories for Quiet Despair

The following accessories are Cool Guy armor:

♦ **Leather Bracelet (fraying slightly):**

 ♦ You've worn it since ... well, no one knows. You don't take it off. Not for showers. Not for heartbreak.
 ♦ It says, "There was a time I believed in permanence."

♦ **Unlabeled Beanie (indoors, always):**

 ♦ It is not for warmth. It's not even for fashion. It's for hiding. For holding. For becoming a concept.
 ♦ It says, "I make music, even if I don't share it," "I've cried in an airport," "Please don't touch my crown chakra."

♦ **Tarnished Ring (not from marriage):**

 ♦ It's worn on an unconventional finger.
 ♦ It's possibly engraved.

* If asked about it, say, "It belonged to someone I used to be." Then change the subject to dreams. Or loss. Or both.

Nonprescription Glasses Worn Intermittently:

* You don't need them; you feel them.
* Put them on when someone asks something real. Take them off when they compliment your smile.

Chain Necklace with One Charm:

* The charm is not centered.
* The chain is not precious metal.
* The meaning is unclear. Could be a locket. A key. A coin. A bullet casing. Could be a metaphor. Probably is.

Notebook with Nothing Written in It:

* It's always visible, but it's not for notes. It's for aura.

* Used for
  * decor on coffee-shop tables
  * pretending you carry it with you to "jot things down"
  * holding the weight of all the things you won't say out loud.

* I once carried a notebook so impractical it didn't even fit in my bag. I lugged it around anyway, like proof I might one day write the thing I kept telling people I was working on. I didn't. But people saw the notebook and nodded. And that was enough.

♦ **The Emotional Accessory Holy Grail:**

  ♦ One item—just one—must feel burdened with memory. When they ask, give them a long pause and a faint, wounded smile, and then murmur: "It's a long story." That's all they get. And that's more than enough.

What Not to Wear

There is absolutely nothing cool about wearing

  ♦ matching sets

  ♦ logos bigger than your abandonment issues

  ♦ smartwatches

    ♦ Nothing screams "I'm thriving" louder than tracking your steps. Remember: You're not thriving; you're brooding.

  ♦ anything that implies you have it together.

    ♦ The more "together" you look, the less mystery there is to mine. And mystery is your only real currency. Cash runs out. Looks fade. But something that suggests a wild summer in Shanghai? That will buy you at least five minutes of attention at any party.

Final Thought

You don't accessorize to impress. You accessorize so people notice the scar without ever seeing the wound.

Let them notice your watch. Let them wonder about the ring. Let them ask if they can read what's in your notebook. Then walk away before they open it.

Coolness is style, sure. But the real secret? It's selective revelation, artfully delayed.

The news sells the apocalypse with a weather graphic and a sponsor's logo. You sell your inner apocalypse with posture and playlists. The scream never leaves. Cool just teaches it to whisper.

Screaming on the Inside

A Guided Visualization

Close your eyes. Now open them—because nothing counts unless someone notices you pretending to heal in public. This is a guided inner scream, designed not to relieve stress but to contain it elegantly. To channel your despair into posture and performative stillness. To be the man who has clearly felt too much ... and learned to say nothing.

Let's begin.

Phase 1: Grounding in the Unbearable Now

Feel your feet. Notice that they are not running. You've chosen to be here—in this party, this café, this temporary job that pays just enough to dull your ambition.

Take one shallow breath. That's enough. Deep breathing shows effort. Because let's be real: I tried meditating once, and all I could think about was whether my ex still listens to the playlist I made.

Effort is suspicious. Shallow is chic.

Look around. Everyone seems fine; that's the illusion. You're not the only one screaming.

You're just the only one doing it tastefully. I sometimes wonder if that's the whole game—turning what feels unbearable into something someone else might misinterpret as poise. Like interior design for emotions: Hide the cracks, put a lamp in the corner, and no one will notice the foundation is shot.

Phase 2: Summoning the Scream

Visualize your internal monologue: unread messages, bad jokes, the time your boss said, "circle back" and you actually circled back but your boss didn't remember asking you to in the first place.

Feel the scream rise—then remember you left laundry in the dryer. That's fine. Fold the despair into the socks.

Store it on the same shelf where you keep every text you decided not to send, and the childhood dream you downgraded into a LinkedIn headline.

Phase 3: The Mask Reset

You're about to re-enter the social field. This requires a recalibration of facial expressions. Choose between the following:

- a dead-eyed smirk

- an "I'm listening, but I'm also dissociating" head tilt

- a faint half-laugh followed by a distant stare toward something you don't actually see

Optional: Check your phone without unlocking it, as if the act itself is the message.

These are the small rituals of emotional invisibility.

Phase 4: Existential Affirmation

Whisper silently to yourself: "No one really knows me. And that's how I like it."

Now, doubt it. Let the doubt harden into posture. Sit straighter. Loosen your jaw. Look like someone who's about to say something important—but won't. Perfect.

Phase 5: Closing the Portal

The scream is still there; you've just taught it to wear better shoes—something resilient enough for despair, stylish enough for lunch at that new café. You will carry the scream with you into the next conversation, the next "vibe," the next performative date.

The scream won't go away, of course. Not really. But maybe the point isn't silence. Maybe the point is to keep it dressed well enough so that no one asks too many questions. And if they do, you can always shrug and change the subject to playlists.

Smile. Say nothing.

Final Thought

You are not healed. You are functioning, artfully. You are coping, stylishly. You are

screaming—on the inside—but with posture that says you could maybe teach yoga, if yoga allowed crying.

And that, my friend, is cool.

Cool In The Wild

A Final Self-Interview,
Conducted in Hindsight,
After the Performance Ends

Q: How can I spot cool in the wild?

A: It's not the loudest guy. It's not the one with the flashy coat. Real cool barely registers until it's gone. You notice it after the person leaves, and suddenly the room feels warmer but a little less interesting. Cool in the wild stands like a fleeting shadow you sensed in the corner of the room. It vanishes when observed too directly, like faith or street parking.

Q: Can women be cool too?

A: Women? Ah, yes. They invented it. Men are just little boys in survival mode, wrapped in layered outfits and odd playlists. Women were cool before we even figured it out. The coolest person I ever met was a woman wearing no makeup, reading a leatherbound book in a crowded restaurant. She didn't even glance up when I passed. I left the place. I didn't belong there. But later, I married her. Long story.

Q: Do you have to be attractive to be cool?

A: No. But you do have to understand angles—physical and emotional. You need good lighting. You need mystery. Look at actors and performers. People expect them to be beautiful, sure. But many of the coolest people aren't beautiful in the traditional sense; they just know how to pause before responding, or how to hold silence like it's something fragile.

Q: Can you be cool, then uncool, then cool again?

A: Yes. Cool is cyclical. You peak, you fall, you disappear, and then one day someone says, "You're looking good," and you realize they mean it. You're not looking good because you tried, but because you stopped trying. Cool returns not with effort, but with exhaustion. When you give up trying to be liked, it sneaks back in like an old friend.

Q: Have I ever felt that I was too cool for a particular scene, or that a scene was too cool for me?

A: Both, within ten minutes. That's the thing about cool: it's unstable. One minute you're the quietest person in the room, and that makes you untouchable. The next, you're the only one who doesn't remember the host's name, and your appetizer order sounds like a cry for help. Which is why I lean against things so often. Balance is tricky when you're improvising.

Q: Has anyone ever called me out and said I was faking being cool?

A: Once. A barista. She said, "You always act like you don't care, but you really do." I laughed, too loudly (so uncool). Knocked over my coffee. That's when I knew she was smarter than I am. And cooler. I tipped 40 percent. I never went back.

Q: Has anybody ever stared at me when I was posing— as if accusing me?

A: Oh, definitely. I've been caught mid-lean, mid-smirk, mid-micro-adjustment of my collar like I was prepping for a *Vanity Fair* photographer who never arrived. Once, at a bookstore, I was flipping through a poetry collection I didn't understand, and someone walked by, looked too long, and shook his head. Not in disgust; in recognition. Like, "You poor bastard. I see what you're doing." He was right, but I held the pose anyway. Sometimes the performance is all you have left.

Q: Have I ever said something clever, and then immediately realized it felt fake?

A: Every day. That's the curse of being verbal with a splash of charm: you say the thing, everyone laughs. Then hours later, in the cereal aisle, you wonder if you came off like a bad performer from a late-night rerun. That's when you determine to go back to letting your silence do the talking. Which works until someone says, "You okay?" and ruins everything.

Q: Do I ever prepare casual anecdotes in advance, just in case someone asks how I'm doing?

A: Yes. I cycle through them like flashcards in a third-grade arithmetic lesson. "Busy, but good." "Trying to unplug more." "Keeping it together, thanks. You?" They're rehearsed enough to sound breezy, but hollow enough to deflect follow-ups. The truth? I'm not doing great. But when I manage to look incredible, that's enough.

Q: Do I ever walk into a place and feel like everyone else is in on some big secret, but I'm not?

A: Absolutely. I walk into rooms where people talk fluently and passionately about things I don't know. I nod like I agree, but I'm actually Googling the acronym they just used. Everyone else seems so sure. But that's what cool is sometimes: highly functioning confusion, styled well and delivered with a smirk.

Q: What's the worst thing someone could say to me in a moment of calm?

A: "You seem really happy." Happiness is too heavy to hold. I'd rather you said nothing. Or had asked more about my weekend in Dubai.

Q: Has anyone ever seen me fully?

A: Before I met my wife, I'd been seen fully just once. The woman who saw through me didn't say it directly. She just watched me talk and then asked, very softly, "Does it ever stop?" I knew exactly what she meant: the pretending, the need to be interesting and clever at all times. At the time, that was the closest I'd come to being known.

Q: What's the uncoolest thing I do regularly?

A: I rehearse phone calls out loud, sometimes while walking. Full lines of dialogue, alternate endings. I pretend I'm smoother than I am. If someone sees me mid-rehearsal, I pretend I'm humming.

Q: Do I ever feel like my own vibe has gone stale?

A: Frequently. You build this persona—cool, low-effort, vaguely haunted—and one day it starts to feel like a costume. The jacket's still good. But something underneath is flat. That's when I smile too much or ask someone a real question. Then I go right back to the old settings, like renewing a bad apartment's lease because the view's still nice.

Q: What scares me more: being boring, or being known?

A: Don't make me choose. Boring is death by shrug. Being known is death by honesty. I'd rather be misunderstood. At least then I can rewrite the story in my head later. You can survive a lot if you stay vague enough.

Q: Do I ever dress for revenge?

A: Always. Every fitted tee, every scent-layered exit is a rebuttal to being underestimated. I've walked into rooms just to haunt someone who once said I was "hard to read." I'm not hard to read. I'm just not letting you hold the book yet.

Q: Have I ever left a party without saying goodbye?

A: Always. Not because I'm rude, but because I can't face the dip in the conversation when I announce I'm leaving. The pause. The polite protests. The look in someone's eyes that says, "We barely noticed you were here." So I ghost. That way, I can pretend someone missed me.

Q: What do I do when someone compliments me?

A: I try to deflect their words with humor or redirect with something like, "This? Oh, it's vintage." I can't take kindness straight. I need it watered down, buffered by sarcasm. If you really want to flatter me, say it quietly so I can pretend I didn't hear you.

Q: Do I ever post something and delete it five minutes later?

A: I once posted a photo that made me look stunning and lonely. I deleted it before anyone could like it. I wanted attention, not exposure. There's a difference.

Q: What's my relationship with silence?

A: Complicated. I crave it, but when I get it, I start performing. I talk to no one, hum to no beat, check my phone just to see a blank screen. Silence makes me audible to myself. Some days, that's too loud.

Q: Do I ever pretend not to see someone in public?

A: Regularly. Not out of cruelty—out of mercy. For both of us. Because sometimes the best version of me is the one you don't talk to. Better to leave me idealized.

Q: What's the coolest lie I've ever told?

A: I once told someone I was "in between ideas." Like creativity was a train I missed, not a thing I'd lost faith in. They nodded, expecting more. I walked away.

Q: Has my cool ever backfired?

A: Of course. I once wore sunglasses indoors to look untouchable and walked straight into a sliding glass door. People laughed. I bowed slightly, like it was performance art.

Q: Do I ever feel like a parody of myself?

A: I live there. I rent monthly. The voice in my head narrates my life like I'm in a streaming series no one finishes. I sometimes say things just to hear how they sound.

Q: What's something I miss that no one talks about?

A: Shared silence that wasn't awkward. When you could sit beside someone and not scroll or speak. That kind of quiet is extinct now. It's been replaced by sharing TikTok videos and social media gossip.

Q: What's my ultimate fear when it comes to being seen?

A: That someone will name the exact thing I'm pretending not to be. That they'll say, "You're trying so hard not to try." They'll be right, and I won't be able to laugh it off. And then what?

Q: Did I ever apologize to my brother for the snowball?

A: No. I didn't. I don't even know if he remembers it the way I do: me standing near the pond, the snowball packed too tight, thrown more like a warning than an assault. It knocked his glasses sideways. He didn't cry. He just looked up like he'd seen something disarming in me. I scrambled down, made a weak excuse, and tried to laugh it off. He shrugged it off too, in that way little brothers do when they're used to you being half hero, half villain. But the damage was done. Not to his head. To whatever trust he still had in me.

I think about it sometimes, especially when I see him now. He's solid, dependable, the kind of man who'd never throw first, even if he could win the fight. The type of man who would've caught me if the roles were reversed. He never brought it up again. I never said I was sorry, but I carry it like I did.

Q: Did my cool mask ever fail?

A: More often than I'd like to admit. It usually starts small: a twitch when someone gets too close to the truth; a silence where a joke should've been; a look that I forgot to disguise. The mask doesn't fall all at once.

When people start to see the outline of something raw underneath, I can't quite pull it back in time.

Q: What causes it to fail?

A: Grief. Real joy. Someone being genuinely kind without wanting anything in return.

Music, sometimes—something I loved to hear when I was young and haven't heard since. Old photos. Watching someone I love walk away. The sound of my daughter's voice when she says something that I've never heard before. And sometimes it slips when I haven't had quite enough sleep, and someone asks me an honest question. Like you just did.

Q: Was it worth it to learn to be cool?

A: That's the kind of question that makes you stop mid-step, stare at your own reflection in a store window, and wonder who you've been performing for all these years. I have no answer.

On the one hand, being cool was a kind of armor. It kept me safe in places where being earnest would've gotten me eaten alive. It gave me distance. Control. A way to walk into a room and not disappear. A way to hide the fact that I didn't always know who I was—only who I didn't want to be. It got me jobs. Lovers. Invitations. Respect I hadn't yet earned. But it also kept people out. Made me suspicious of sincerity. Taught me to dodge intimacy like it was a punch.

So ... was it worth it? Sometimes. But the better question is: do I still need it? And that answer's changing. Maybe.

Are You
Cool on the Outside,
Screaming on the Inside?

A Self-Assessment You Didn't Ask For

Some quizzes try to help you grow. This one just wants you to notice the quiet hum of dread underneath your latest jacket purchase. Be honest when answering the below questions. (If you lie to a questionnaire, what else are you lying to? Just wondering.)

1. Have you ever searched "haircuts for men over fifty" while pretending you were reading political news?
   ❑ Yes
   ❑ No

2. Have you ever said "vibe check" in a room where the vibe immediately collapsed?
   ❑ Yes
   ❑ No

3. Do you own twenty-seven shirts, but only three of them pass your personal panic test?
   ❑ Yes
   ❑ No

4. Have you ever said, "Back in my day ..." and then audibly sighed?
   - ❑Yes
   - ❑No

5. Do you have a skincare routine that mostly exists in theory and/or in drawer clutter?
   - ❑Yes
   - ❑No

6. Does TikTok make you feel like you're being chased in a language you no longer speak?
   - ❑Yes
   - ❑No

7. Has a Gen Z colleague ever called you "sir" (and you still haven't recovered)?
   - ❑Yes
   - ❑No

8. Have you ever sniffled when listening to a song from your high school days and blamed it on allergies?
   - ❑Yes
   - ❑No

9. Do you often scan the room and realize you're the only one who remembers rotary phones and snack cakes that tasted like chemicals?
   - ❑Yes
   - ❑No

10. Do you sometimes feel like the last human alive who took Y2K seriously?
    - ❏ Yes
    - ❏ No

11. Do you look at modern fashion and wonder if it's revenge for something your generation did?
    - ❏ Yes
    - ❏ No

12. True or False: You don't know who the current top ten performing artists are. (You say it proudly, but it stings.)
    - ❏ True
    - ❏ False

13. True or False: You haven't been to a dance club since the Bush administration (either one).
    - ❏ True
    - ❏ False

14. If asked to dance on the spot, would your brain shut down and reboot in safe mode?
    - ❏ Yes
    - ❏ No

15. Do you act like you're not checking your reflection in storefront windows?
    - ❏ Yes
    - ❏ No

16. Have you opened a retirement account and then immediately bought running sneakers even though you don't run?

    ❑ Yes

    ❑ No

17. Do AARP mailers arrive with your name pre-printed?

    ❑ Yes

    ❑ No

18. Are you looking forward to getting a senior sticker for free parking at the municipal lot?

    ❑ Yes

    ❑ No

19. Do strangers sometimes hold the door for you (and you hate how nice it feels)?

    ❑ Yes

    ❑ No

20. Have you ever imagined owning a cane (just out of curiosity)?

    ❑ Yes

    ❑ No

21. Have you ever said, "LOL" out loud and watched a Gen Z barista's soul leave their body?

    ❑ Yes

    ❑ No

22. Have you ever dropped a pop culture reference that landed like a PowerPoint error message?

 ❏ Yes

 ❏ No

23. Do you still wear sneakers you bought in 2008 because they're "classic" and bordering on vintage now?

 ❏ Yes

 ❏ No

24. Do you nap now?

 ❏ Yes

 ❏ No

25. When you see old friends, is the first thing you discuss your latest medical report?

 ❏ Yes

 ❏ No

Score your answers

(Yes/True = 1 point, No/False = 0 points)

and see which cool category you fall into.

0–7: Vintage Confidence or Strategic Denial: You either have the emotional metabolism of a Greek god or you're holding back a midlife monsoon behind those vintage sunglasses. Either way, respect.

8–15: Cracks in the Chrome: You're self-aware, emotionally limber, and possibly hoarding moisturizer samples. Cool still fits, but some seams are fraying—mostly on the inside.

16–22: The Style-Stress Equilibrium Is Wobbling: You've learned to fake chill while quietly spiraling during hold music. Your style remains intact. Your playlists are haunted. You've stopped explaining references—not just because they don't land, but because it hurts when they don't.

23–25: You are Cool on the Outside, Screaming on the Inside: You walk into rooms like you still belong there, even though you're scanning for exits and avoiding mirrors. Your cool is earned. Your screaming is dignified. You've faced midlife uncertainty—and you are still standing.

In business, cool is outlasting the boss everyone hates. At home, love is outlasting the arguments until you're laughing about them. Same skill. Different battlefields. Cool cracks eventually; the trick is knowing what's worth rebuilding.

When Cool Meets We

So now I'm in a relationship. A real one. Not a "situation," and not with someone who leaves their toothbrush but won't commit to a weekend away together. This is someone who knows my middle name, my coffee order, and my moods. This isn't a vibe. Basically, it's IKEA with emotions.

I've slipped past the event horizon of solitude and woken up in orbit around a shared life. There are joint calendars. A shared Spotify account. Even a mortgage. We smile at dinner parties like we're not silently judging what the hosts serve for appetizers.

And somehow it works.

This isn't the cool I started with. It's not the curated detachment, the razor-sharp aesthetic, the emotionally minimalist armor I wrapped around my pain like a second skin. This is messier. Quieter. More exposed.

Sometimes I catch myself carrying a vacuum up the stairs and think, "This is it. This is adulthood. No leather jacket, no ironic playlist. Just me, sweating, trying not to dent the banister." And yet that's somehow better than all the moody posturing combined.

This is the cool that does dishes. The cool that texts, "I'm picking up something for dinner." How did I get here?

I don't know, honestly. There was a time when "connection" sounded like a trap, like an airport layover I didn't plan for. But somehow, I blinked, and here I was, arguing about window hardware like it was a competitive sport. It snuck up on me: domesticity. And then I realized it isn't an enemy at all. It's just another space to be cool in, if you're willing to learn the choreography. The cool that apologizes first. The cool that laughs at itself.

And when it works—when you both drop the performance long enough to meet in the middle—it's better than cool; it's connection.

If you've made it this far, you're not just surviving. You're building. And that might be the most radical thing of all.

Can We Be Cool Together?

*A Q&A with a Man Who Somehow
Got a Second Chance at Love*

Q: You're in a real relationship now. Are you still cool?

A: At best, sustainably lukewarm. She mistakes my blank stares for depth, which is love in action.

Q: Do you still have routines?

A: I meditate, but now there's a dog involved. I still cook eggs on Sunday, but we argue about the playlist. There are woven baskets, too. I've made peace with it.

Q: Do you fight?

A: Yes. But calmly. Less like a battle, more like a slow-motion eye roll. I'm learning to say what's wrong. It's deeply uncool, but apparently better for longevity.

Q: Have you changed?

A: I think so. I text back quickly. I let her choose the movie without performing visible martyrdom. I think that counts.

Cool with Kids

*Surviving Playdates, Soccer Sidelines, and
Snack Duty without Losing Your Identity*

Q: Can cool survive Goldfish and tantrums?

A: Not in its original form. I've traded aloof detachment
for mastery of the car seat buckle. That's evolution.

Q: What if you become the snack parent?

A: I own it. I elevate it. I cut fruit into squares and call
it design. I bring vegan snacks to soccer practice in
order to score points with the trendy parents. I lose
the points when they discover that I brought Oreos,
but who cares? The kids say I'm the cool dad now.
And I am.

Q: Can your kid be cooler than you?

A: My daughter listens to cheerful European dance
remixes of songs that were once sad. Sometimes I
stand outside her door just to remind myself that I used
to know what I liked. She's cooler than I ever was. My
only hope is that she doesn't realize it before college.

How to Argue Without Looking Uncool in Front of Your Wife's Friends

The Quiet Art of Saving Face While Apologizing with Your Whole Chest

Q: They take her side. Do you defend yourself?

A: No. I listen. I use self-deprecating humor. I wait to make my real point three days later in the kitchen, delivering it casually while slicing cucumbers.

Q: Final verdict: Can you still be cool while being seen this fully?

A: Maybe not everyone thinks so. But if she thinks I'm cool, that's more than enough.

Marriage, Mortgages, and the Myth of Settling Down Gracefully

When Cool Becomes a Co-Signer

Q: Does joint homeownership kill cool?

A: Not kill it, just remodel it. I started choosing closet fixtures and said things like, "This ceiling light feels aggressive." It changed me.

Q: How do you keep the spark?

A: I fold the laundry without being asked. I remember the name of her least favorite coworker. I forget the recycling, though, and she sighs like it's the end of civilization. It isn't—but cool has its limits.

Q: How do you handle it when, say, you have a couple's beach day with your sort-of-friends and someone brings trauma instead of music?

A: I'd spend forty minutes walking through the sand, pretending I dropped my sunglasses.

Q: Final takeaway?

A: Ordinary isn't failure. Sometimes it's the prize. And maybe that's the hardest part to admit: that cool, when shared, stops being armor and starts being furniture. Not sharp. Not performative. Just useful, familiar, lived in. Which is its own kind of radical.

A Final Note from the Author

If you've read this book and felt exposed, misunderstood, or personally attacked, I want you to know that was not my intention. My intention was worse. I wanted you to laugh—and then quietly wonder if I was writing about you.

To anyone I've ghosted … I'm sorry. Unless I forgot. Then, I guess, sorry for forgetting to be sorry. This book is not a defense. It's a confession disguised as a guide. If anything, it's the notes I wish I'd written to myself years ago, back when I thought aloofness was survival instead of camouflage. It worked, for a while. But camouflage has a way of blending you out of your own life.

I've grown. Slightly. I now own a throw pillow. Two, if you count the one I accidentally stole from an Airbnb.

Turns out Mrs. Brown was right. I did have issues. Just not the ones she thought. And somehow, someone married me anyway.

My brother Luke went another way: He's a Bro. Tank tops, tequila, and motivational slogans that sound like protein shakes. He says it works. I say cool was the only mask I could keep from slipping.

—Brand Mavrick

Creative Director (allegedly), Panopticon Agency

Acknowledgments

A special acknowledgment to everyone who is still searching for their way in a world that too easily mistakes glitter for substance.

Thanks to my parents, Charles and Edith, who tried to show me the difference; and to my wife, Liuliang Qin, whose support and encouragement are equal parts ballast and tailwind—and who reminds me when I forget.

Thanks also to Shannon Irving, up in the "Live Free or Die" state (no, Brand didn't coin that slogan, though he wishes he had), for her excellent editorial assistance; and to Lance Buckley for his sharp eye and steady hand in design.

—Charlie O'Neill

About the Authors

BRAND MAVRICK is an agency creative director, part-time human being, and full-time emotional diversion specialist. At the Panopticon Agency in New York, he leads campaigns for brands unsure of their identities but certain of their budgets. His work has been described as "iconic," "disruptive," and "a cry for help disguised as a Super Bowl ad."

He lives with his wife, daughter, brother, and mother in Darien, Connecticut. They share a dog and an overengineered irrigation system.

Brand never planned to write a book. He started jotting down notes on coolness during a long, weaponized silence in a meeting and never stopped. He believes everyone is faking it—some with better playlists, some with better jawlines. He calls himself "comfortable with discomfort," "in therapy, sort of," and "probably just passing through." He splits his time between Darien, New York, existential dread, and any available wall.

This is his first book. It won't be his last if someone offers him a deal; he's already outlined *Sorry I Left Without Saying Goodbye: The Lost Art of Vanishing Gracefully*. But you won't find him on Instagram, or even in real life—because neither he nor the Panopticon Agency exists. Brand Mavrick and Philbert T. Upton are the inventions of **CHARLIE O'NEILL**, who once lived in Darien but now lives in Massachusetts.